WELCOME!

This book stars the pairs of numbers that add to Ten.

These pairs of numbers get their own book because they are so important. Why? Because we have a base-Ten number system, so exciting things happen when you add to Ten.

Because our number system is based on groups of Ten, it's key for children to understand how a group of Ten is formed and to recognize when a group of Ten has been formed. Of course, the sooner this skill becomes internalized, the sooner a child is ready for more advanced math concepts.

Psst... Adding to 10 is easy. Only a few pairs of numbers sum to 10.

You can do it!

TEN FRIENDS

1 + 9 or 9 + 1 = 10
2 + 8 or 8 + 2 = 10
3 + 7 or 7 + 3 = 10
4 + 6 or 6 + 4 = 10
5 + 5 = 10

TEN FRIENDS
Save the Day!

Created & Written by Marty Epstein
Illustrated & Designed by Darrin Pepe
Edited by Mario Garnsworthy

Thanks to:

Casey and Derek for reminding me how much I love math; my family and awesome friends; and Oly, my dog, and his new pal, Vigor, for their unwavering love as well as for being role models of fierce determination and an ever-playful spirit.

- Marty Epstein

About the Author

Marty became concerned about math education when her own children struggled in math at top public schools. Although able to help her sons, who have continued high-level math studies, she realized most children who run into such hiccups would not be so fortunate. Marty started tutoring and substitute teaching in math and was distressed to find key math building blocks missing among so many children. This led to the "aha" realization that this issue is pervasive, altering the future of millions of children. This book series is her way of helping by establishing and strengthening key math building blocks in a fun way. Marty graduated *magna cum laude* from Williams College. She has a PhD in Math Education (UMass Dartmouth) and an MBA (Harvard).

PURPLE PEAKS PRESS

NOTICE OF RIGHTS

By virtue of purchasing this book, limited permission is granted to the classroom teacher to reproduce portions of this work for use only with his or her students. Other than as noted above, this book may not be reproduced or quoted in whole or in part without permission from Purple Peaks Press LLC.©

Text and Illustrations Copyright © 2022 Purple Peaks Press LLC
The Dog Logo is a Trademark of Purple Peaks Press LLC
www.SmilingDogMath.com
Text by Martha Epstein - Illustrations by Darrin Pepe
All Rights Reserved. Printed in the United States
ISBN- 10: 0-997 1266-2-0
ISBN- 13: 978-0-9971266-2-4

TEN FRIENDS
Save the Day!

The NUMBERS and Cousin 10 were eager, excited, thrilled, and delighted. They'd never ridden a roller coaster before. They could hardly wait!

6 + ___ = 10   7 + ___ = 10
8 + ___ = 10   9 + ___ = 10

The NUMBERS sighed, slumped, moped, and moaned.
"I want to ride the roller coaster!" 1 whined.

How many more flowers do you need to make 10 flowers?
____ + ____ = 10

How many stones on the path?

____ big stones + ____ small stones = 10 total stones

"Who needs pears at a time like this!" said 0.
"We do!" said 7, "But, not the kind you eat, the kind that add to 10. Pair up in pairs that add to 10. Then we can ride the roller coaster."

10 + 0, 9 + 1, 8 + 2, 7 + 3, and 6 + 4, strolled onto the roller coaster. But, the man stopped 5.

Sorry. You need 5 + 5 to equal 10.

To ride the roller coaster, each number must team up to add to 10.

Draw a line to connect the number on the left to the number on the right to make pairs of numbers that add to 10. What number does 5 need to find? _____

15

Use this page to solve the problem.

The ride finished. "Eureka! I've got it," said 5. "I just need to pair up with another pair — a pair that adds to five."

Again, again, again, and again, the NUMBERS and Cousin 10 rode the roller coaster. And the day ended up adding up to a pefect 10.

0 + 10. 10 + 0. We make 10. 10's our hero.
1 + 9. 9 + 1. We make 10. It's so fun!
2 + 8. 8 + 2. We make 10. So can you.
3 + 7. 7 + 3. We make 10, easily.
4 + 6. 6 + 4. We make 10, and not one more.
5 + 5. Add 5 twice. We make 10. Wow! That's nice.

TEN FRIENDS
Save the Day!
★ ACTIVITIES ★

ADD TO 10

Which pairs of numbers add together to make the number in the star? Draw a curved line to connect them.

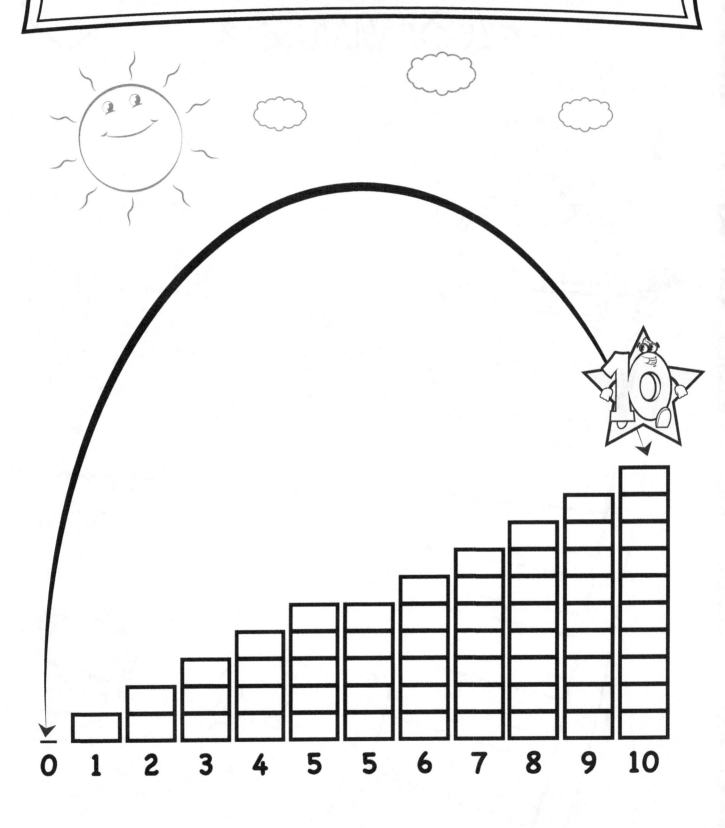

Add up the numbers and draw a line to the answer.

1 + 2
3 + 3
4 + 2
1 + 2
1 + 4
3 + 2
5 + 1
2 + 2
4 + 1
2 + 4
1 + 3
2 + 1
2 + 3
1 + 5
1 + 1
3 + 1

HELP EVERYONE HAVE 10 LOLLIPOPS!
Draw a line to connect the number of lollipops on the left to the number on the right to make a group of 10 lollipops.

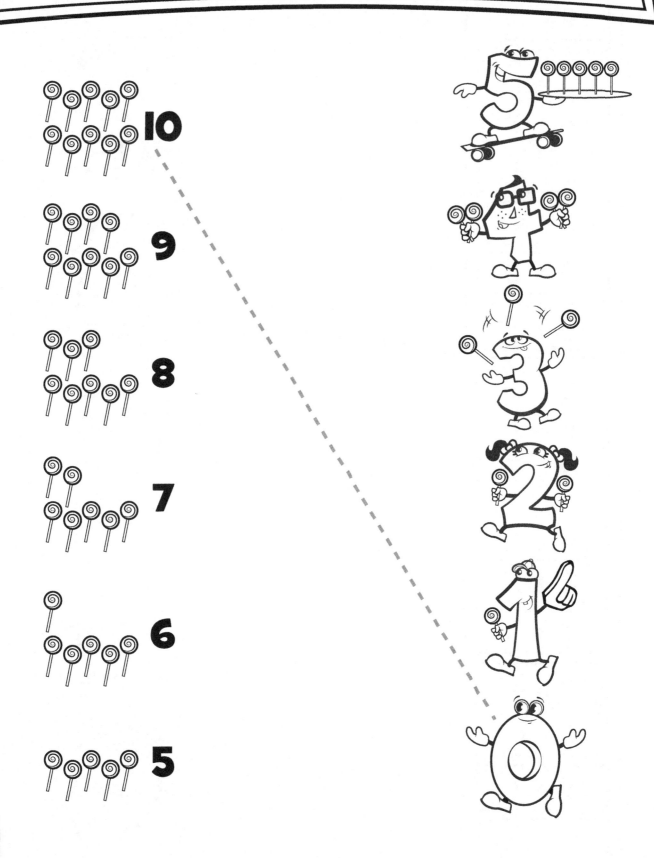

HELP EVERYONE HAVE 10 LOLLIPOPS!
Draw a line to connect the number of lollipops on the left to the number on the right to make a group of 10 lollipops.

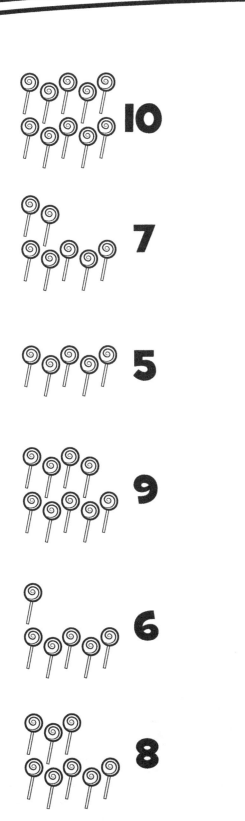

ADD TO 10!
The numbers need to be in pairs that add to 10.
Draw in the missing numbers.

33

Add up the numbers and draw a line to the answer.

- 1 + 7
- 5 + 4
- 3 + 5
- 8 + 1
- 3 + 6
- 7 + 2
- 5 + 3
- 4 + 5
- 3 + 4
- 1 + 8
- 5 + 4
- 4 + 3
- 2 + 7
- 4 + 4
- 6 + 3

It's okay if it's hard sometimes.

Practice makes it easier.

I love it when things add up.

You guessed it. The numbers need to be in pairs that add to 10 to ride the roller coaster. Draw in the missing numbers: 0, 1, 2, 3, 4, and 5.

Fill in the missing numbers.

10

DING! DING!

- 10 + ___ = 10
- 9 + ___ = 10
- 8 + ___ = 10
- 7 + ___ = 10
- 6 + ___ = 10
- 5 + ___ = 10
- 4 + ___ = 10
- 3 + ___ = 10
- 2 + ___ = 10
- 1 + ___ = 10
- 0 + ___ = 10

Fill in the missing numbers.

10

9 + ___ = 10

1 + ___ = 10

8 + ___ = 10

2 + ___ = 10

7 + ___ = 10

3 + ___ = 10

6 + ___ = 10

4 + ___ = 10

5 + ___ = 10

10 + ___ = 10

0 + ___ = 10

Fill in the roller coaster cars with the pairs of numbers that add to 10. One number needs to be counted twice. Which one is that?

Create your own adding-to-10 activities.

Create your own adding-to-10 activities.

TEN FRIENDS Save The Day! ANSWER PAGE

Page 26
Page 27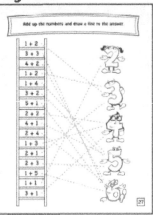
Page 28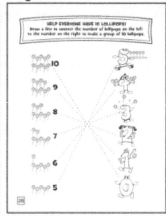
Page 29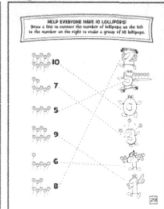

Page 30
Page 31
Page 32
Page 33

Page 34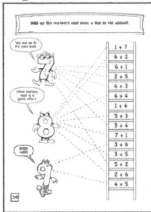
Page 35
Page 36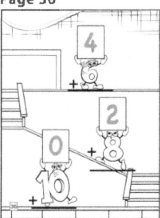
Page 37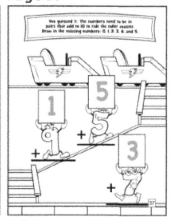

Page 38
Page 39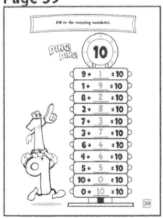
Page 40
Page 41

Made in the USA
Coppell, TX
08 June 2025

50468676R00031